Foundations

A LEVEL Manuscript Workbook

Denise Eide

LogicofEnglish®

Foundations Level A Manuscript Workbook
by Logic of English®

Logic of English, Inc
4865 19th Street NW, Suite 130
Rochester, MN 55901

Cover Designer & Illustrator: Ingrid Hess
Royalty Free Images: Shutterstock
LOE School Font: David Occhino Design

ISBN 978-1-936706-32-7

First Edition

20 19 18 17 16 15 14 13

www.logicofenglish.com

LESSON 1

Name _____

1.1 Compound Words

1.2 Optional Handwriting Chart

A.2 Handwriting

LESSON **6**

Name _____

6.1 One-Syllable Words

Name _____

d

d

d

d

LESSON 7

Name _____

7.1 Beginning Sounds

LESSON 8

8.1 Beginning Sounds

g

g

g

g

g

g

g

a

d

d

g

a

8.4 Handwriting Practice

Name _____

g

g

g

g

LESSON 9

Name _____

9.1 Beginning Sounds

g   a

a   d

c   g

d   c

C

C

C

C

LESSON 10

Name _____

10.1 Segmenting Words

g

o

c

d

a

a

c

d

g

o

O

O

O

O

ASSESSMENT B Name _____

B.1 One-Syllable Words

1. | a | g | o | d |

2. | g | c | a | o |

3. | c | d | o | a |

4. | a | c | d | g |

5. | o | d | c | a |

LESSON **11**

Name _____

11.1 Guess the Animal

Name _____

𝓁

𝓁

𝓁

𝓁

LESSON 12

Name _____

12.1 Guess the Food

Name _____

12.3 Handwriting Practice   Name _____

qu

qu

qu

qu

LESSON 13

Name _____

13.1 Segmenting Words

13.2 Handwriting Practice   Name _____

ꕷ

ꕷ

ꕷ

ꕷ

a	qu	d
g	c	o
o	d	qu

d	a	o
g	qu	c
c	d	qu

g	a	d
a	qu	g
d	c	o

g	d	c
g	c	qu
a	o	d

LESSON 14

Name _____

14.1 Matching Phonograms

s	g
g	o
a	qu
qu	s
o	a

_S_

_S_

S

S

LESSON 15

Name _____

15.1 Handwriting Practice

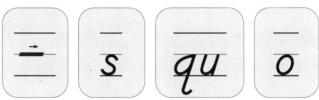

ASSESSMENT C   Name _____

C.1 One-Syllable Words

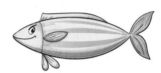

Name _____

a c d g o qu s

1. | c | g | a | s |

2. | a | d | qu | o |

3. | o | d | g | s |

4. | qu | g | a | o |

5. | s | a | c | qu |

6. | c | a | s | g |

7. | a | d | c | g |

LESSON 16

Name _____

16.1 The Phonogram t

16.2 Handwriting Practice   Name _____

$\dagger$

$\dagger$

$\dagger$

$\dagger$

LESSON 17

Name _____

17.1 Blending

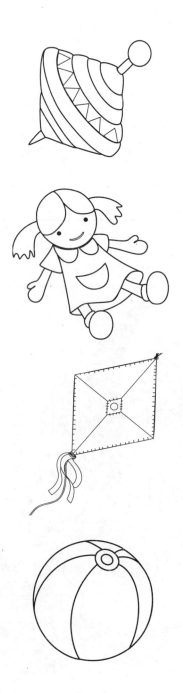

t	qu
qu	i
g	t
i	a
d	g
a	d

i

i

i

i

a	*d*	*g*
c	*t*	*qu*
s	*o*	*i*

17.4 Phonogram Bingo continued

t	s	i
qu	o	g
c	a	d

LESSON 18

Name _____

18.1 Phonograms at the Beginning of Words

a   d   g

i   d   g

a   d   g

o   t   s

a   qu   i

qu   d   a

18.1 Phonograms at the Beginning of Words continued

t   g   s

d   i   qu

i   c   qu

c   o   i

g   c   t

s   o   i

d   o   c

s   d   a

18.2 Handwriting Practice

Name _____

ᗡ↓

ᗡ↓

ᗡ↓

ᗡ↓

LESSON 19

Name _____

19.1 Phonograms at the Beginning of Words

a   i   o

t   s   g

t   qu   g

a   g   d

d   g   qu

qu   c   i

19.1 Phonograms at the Beginning of Words continued

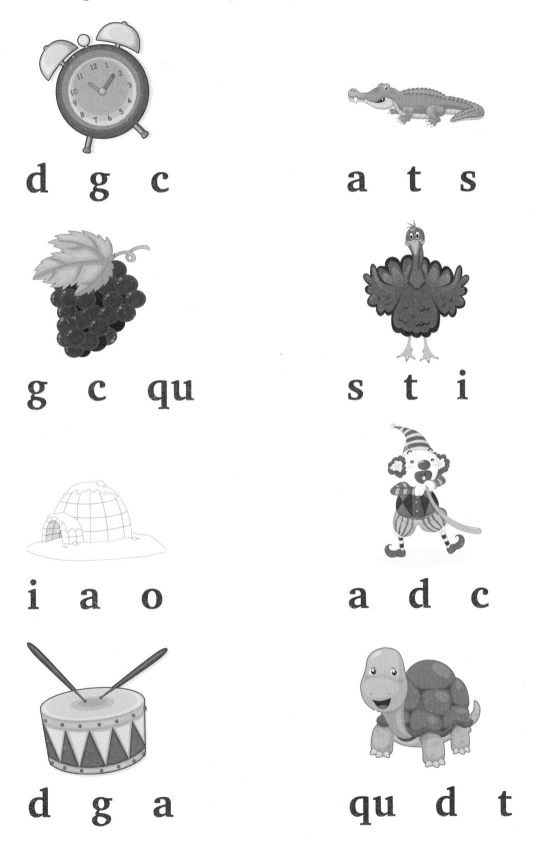

d g c   a t s

g c qu   s t i

i a o   a d c

d g a   qu d t

19.2 Handwriting Practice

Name _____

p

p

p

p

c	g	s
d	qu	t
o	p	i

p	qu	o
c	a	g
i	s	t

LESSON 20

Name _____

20.1 Sounds at the End of Words

t	s
u	g
s	p
p	t
i	u
g	i

20.3 Handwriting Practice

Name _____

U

U

U

U

ASSESSMENT **D** Name _____

D.1 Beginning Sounds

c　g　t

t　s　g

a　t　s

a　p　s

a　c　d

d　u　i

Name _____

p   s   t   i   qu   u

1. c qu a g

2. p d a g

3. a u o i

4. d s a u

5. g qu t u

6. u p s i

LESSON 21

Name _____

21.1 Listening for Sounds at the End of Words

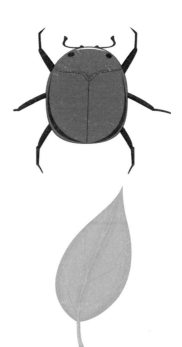

j

j

j

j

cat

sad

pig

pot

LESSON 22

Name _____

22.1 Handwriting Practice

w

w

w

w

Name _____

pup

cup

tag

cat

LESSON 23

23.1 Matching Phonograms

w	s
u	g
s	j
j	w
g	u

dig

dog

jug

wig

cup

cop

cap

cat

LESSON 24

Name _____

24.1 Identify the Phonogram at the End of a Word

c   t   s

t   j   g

a   d   t

s   g   j

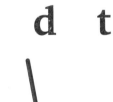

c   p   d

a   t   g

Name _____

LESSON 25

Name _____

25.1 Identify the Phonogram at the End of a Word

s   t   g

c   p   d

c   t   s

t   j   g

a   r   t

r   a   p

r

r

r

r

ASSESSMENT E

E.1 Identify the Phonogram at the End of a Word

c   t   j

a   r   t

c   t   s

a   g   w

w   j   d

p   a   g

Name _____

t i p u j w r

1.   d   u   i   a

2.   j   p   t   w

3.   p   d   j   r

4.   i   r   d   s

5.   t   d   i   p

6. 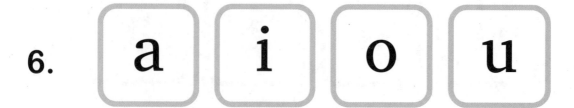 a i o u

7. w u c g

Name _____

rug

pot

dog

rat

cup

cat

sit

rod

LESSON 26

Name _____

26.1 Handwriting Practice

n

n

n

n

cups

pin

cup

pins

dog

dogs

pig

pigs

LESSON 27

Name _____

27.1 Handwriting Practice

m _____

m _____

m _____

m _____

Name _____

m	qu	r	w
d	n	j	u
g	t	i	p
c	a	s	o

j	t	n	g
w	m	c	p
o	u	a	i
qu	r	s	d

dog and cat

cat and rat

cat on rug

pigs and mud

LESSON 28

Name _____

28.1 Handwriting Practice

LESSON 29

Name _____

29.1 Phonograms in the Middle of the Word

a   i   u

u   a   i

i   a   u

u   o   i

a   i   u

u   a   o

e

e

e

e

spin	run
stop	sit
stand	jump
stomp	snap
drop	jog
tap	trip
dig	pat
tug	step

29.3 Read and Do continued

game	game
game	game
game	game
game	game
game	game
game	game
game	game
game	game

LESSON 30

Name _____

30.1 Handwriting Practice

Name _____

e   **a**   u

a   i   u

o   **a**   u

u   a   **e**

a   **i**   u

u   e   a

ASSESSMENT F

Name _____

F.1 Phonograms in the Middle of the Word

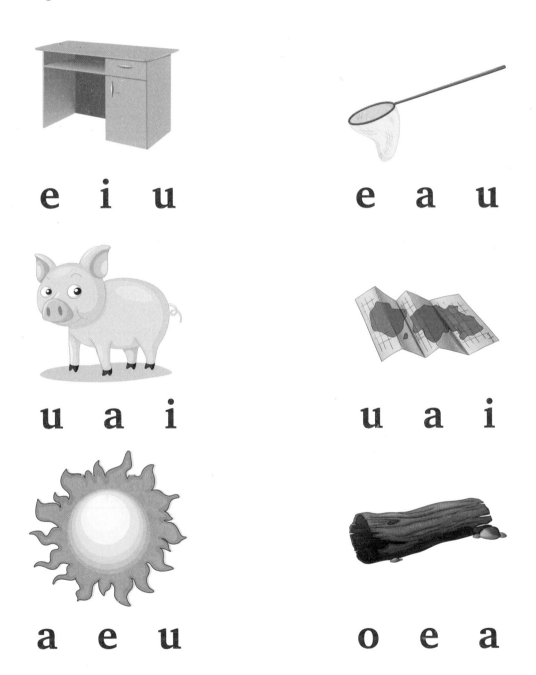

e   i   u

e   a   u

u   a   i

u   a   i

a   e   u

o   e   a

j w r n m l e

1. j   w   i   e

2. l   r   t   u

3. a   e   j   r

4. i   r   w   l

5. m   n   t   r

6. u a w e

7. l m n o

Name _____

red cup

pot and lid

cat and rat

wet mop

LESSON 31

31.1 Sounds at the Beginning of Words

31.2 Handwriting Practice   Name _____

b

b

b

b

and	band
bend	spend
land	sand
stand	brand
lend	mend
pond	send
tend	wind
blend	grand

31.3 Reading Basketball

game

game

game

game

game

game

game

game

game

game

game

game

game

game

game

game

LESSON **32**

Name _____

32.1 Sounds at the Beginning of Words

h	e
b	g
s	h
g	l
l	s
e	b

Name _____

h

h

h

h

LESSON 33

Name _____

33.1 Handwriting Practice

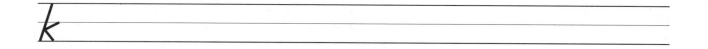

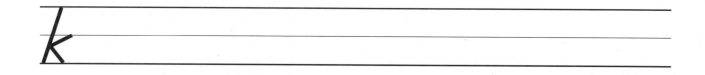

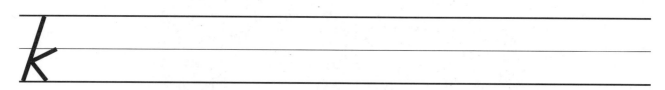

wink

sink

pond

hot sand

pink hat

big log

red tent

red bug

big jet

big bed

33.3 Blending Game

st	sp
sm	sn
sk	sw
bl	cl
tw	gl
pl	sl
br	cr
dr	tr
gr	pr

33.3 Blending Game

blends	blends
blends	blends
blends	blends
blends	blends
blends	blends
blends	blends
blends	blends
blends	blends
blends	blends

Name _____

Blends

LESSON 34

Name _____

34.1 Handwriting Practice

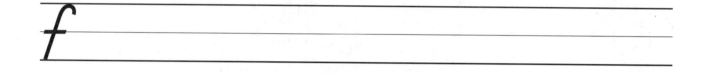

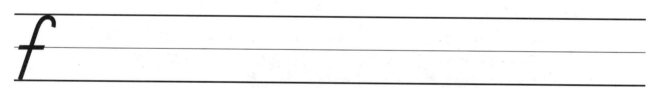

nd	nk
nt	mp
stop	snap
flap	flat
clap	glad
plan	slam
drip	drop
drink	trip
trap	trot

34.2 Blending Game

blends	blends
blends	blends
blends	blends
blends	**blends**
blends	**blends**
blends	**blends**
blends	blends
blends	blends
blends	blends

LESSON 35

Name _____

35.1 Multi-Syllable Words

v	f
b	l
f	v
r	s
l	r
s	b

V

V

V

V

vest	mad
frog	sad
cat	dad
dog	mom
skunk	sink
milk	fan
bat	hot
bag	pig
sand	gum

35.4 Charades

game

game

game

game

game

game

game

game

game

game

game

game

game

game

game

game

game

game

ASSESSMENT G Name _____

G.1 Phonemic Awareness

bat

__at

__at

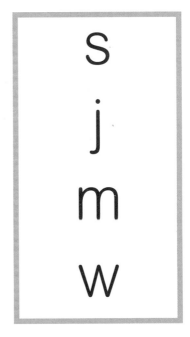

Name _____

$\overline{n}$ $\overline{m}$ $\overline{e}$ $\overline{l}$ $\overline{b}$ $\overline{h}$ $\overline{k}$ $\overline{f}$ $\overline{v}$

1. b j h d

2. h i l t

3. h n e u

4. k r w m

5. m e c d

6. w f t g

7. o v u w

8. r s h p

9. qu l t k

Name _____

hot pot

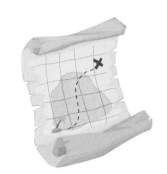

wet net

bad map

big bag

pink fan

nest

hand

wet sink

pink bus

LESSON 36

Name _____

36.1 Handwriting Practice

_X_

_X_

_X_

_X_

fast fox

big box

red van

fat frog

tan lamp

an	and
am	ask
at	best
big	but
can	cut
did	fast
get	got
had	him
hot	if

36.3 High-Frequency Words

High-Frequency Words

High-Frequency Words

High-Frequency Words

High-Frequency Words

High-Frequency Words

High-Frequency Words

High-Frequency Words

High-Frequency Words

High-Frequency Words

High-Frequency Words

High-Frequency Words

High-Frequency Words

High-Frequency Words

High-Frequency Words

High-Frequency Words

High-Frequency Words

High-Frequency Words

High-Frequency Words

LESSON 37

Name _____

37.1 Short Vowel Sounds

y

y

y

y

red	gum
tan	bed
wet	box
hot	cat
big	dog
fun	rat
flat	man
mint	pot
fat	pig

37.3 Phrases

game game

game game

game game

game game

game game

game game

game game

game game

game game

LESSON 38

38.1 Long and Short Vowel Sounds

ē

ă

ū

ĭ

ā

z

z

Z

Z

38.3 Phonogram Board Game

Start

End

in	it
jump	just
let	must
not	on
ran	red
run	sit
six	stop
ten	up
us	went

38.4 High-Frequency Words

High-Frequency Words

High-Frequency Words

High-Frequency Words

High-Frequency Words

High-Frequency Words

High-Frequency Words

High-Frequency Words

High-Frequency Words

High-Frequency Words

High-Frequency Words

High-Frequency Words

High-Frequency Words

High-Frequency Words

High-Frequency Words

High-Frequency Words

High-Frequency Words

High-Frequency Words

High-Frequency Words

LESSON 39

39.1 Short and Long Vowel Sounds

ĭ	ē
ū	ō
ā	ī
ŏ	ĕ
ă	ŭ

z	t	c	i
d	y	u	a
qu	n	r	l
w	m	p	v

r	i	v	m
z	w	a	u
d	qu	p	t
y	n	c	l

ASSESSMENT H

Name _____

H.1 Short and Long Vowel Sounds

ă

ĭ

ē

ĕ

ā

Name _____

b h k f v x y z

1. j   b   i   d

2. l   f   t   g

3. a   e   i   h

4. k   t   p   o

5. w   m   n   v

6. x j b z

7. c y j g

8. z y n a

Name _____

wet mop

tan box

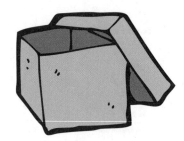

tan hat

hot pot

hot sun

mad crab

pink pig

red flag

dim lamp

mint gum

cup

Pig!

Reader 1

Foundations

LEVEL **A**

Logic of English

jug

11

tag

2

dog

10

wig

3

dig

9

dad

4

cat

pig

cop

7

cap

6

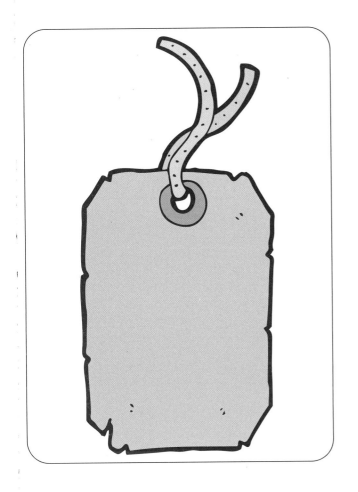

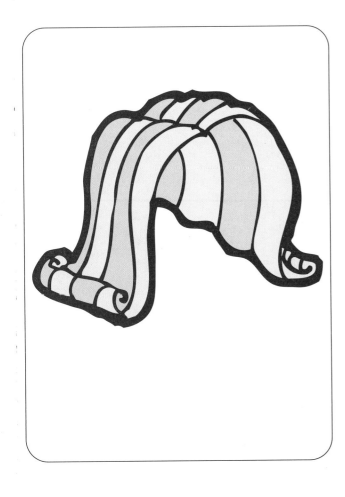

Dogs and Cats!

Reader 2

cat in cup

11

dog and map

2

dog in pot

cat and rat

dog on rug

9

wig on dog

4

cat on rug

wig on cat

tag on cat

6

tag on dog

7

Reader 3

Dogs, Cats, and Rats!

Foundations

LEVEL A

LogicofEnglish®

dog and gum

11

cat and pot

2

rat on log

dog and pan

rat on pig

cat in tent

mud on dog

8

rat in cup

5

cat and rat

rat and dog

Reader 4

Dogs and Cats 2!

bag on dog

hat on cat

wet dog

hat on dog

wet cat

9

dog in hat

4

dogs and cat in bed

cat in hat

cats in bed

dogs in bed

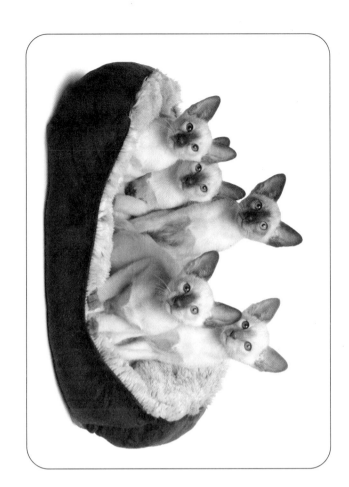

Kids

Reader 5

wet mom, wet dad, and wet kids

hats on glad kids

kids hug

kids on bus

kids in tent

9

kids run fast

4

mom, dad, and
kids sit

glad kids on rug

mom, dad, and kids plant

7

kids stand on sand

6

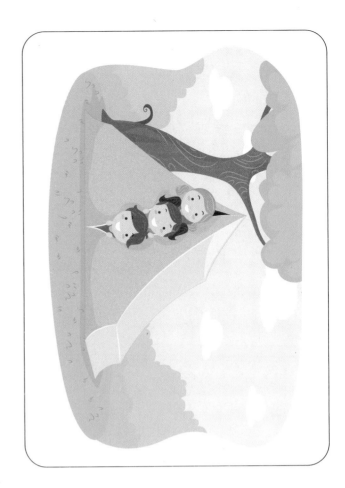

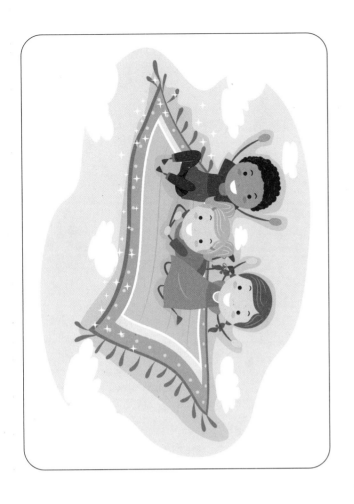

Foundations

A LEVEL

Logic of English

Reader 6

Fun Dogs
Fun Pups

pups in hats

11

pups at vet

2

dog in hat and wig

dog in fins

six pups in box

pup tugs

dog and pom poms

pup naps

wet pup in tub

7

dog mops

6